zendoodle coloring presents

BIRDS IN THE FOREST

AN ARTIST'S COLORING BOOK

★ DENYSE KLETTE ★

CASTLE POINT BOOKS
NEW YORK

ZENDOODLE COLORING PRESENTS BIRDS IN THE FOREST.

Printed in Canada. For information, address
St. Martin's Publishing Group, 120 Broadway, New York, NY 10271.

www.castlepointbooks.com

The Castle Point Books trademark is owned by Castle Point Publishing, LLC.
Castle Point books are published and distributed by St. Martin's Publishing Group.

ISBN 978-1-250-28157-9 (trade paperback)

Our books may be purchased in bulk for promotional, educational, or business use.
Please contact your local bookseller or the Macmillan Corporate and Premium
Sales Department at 1-800-221-7945, extension 5442, or by email
at MacmillanSpecialMarkets@macmillan.com.

First Edition: 2023

10 9 8 7 6 5 4 3 2 1

This book belongs to

....

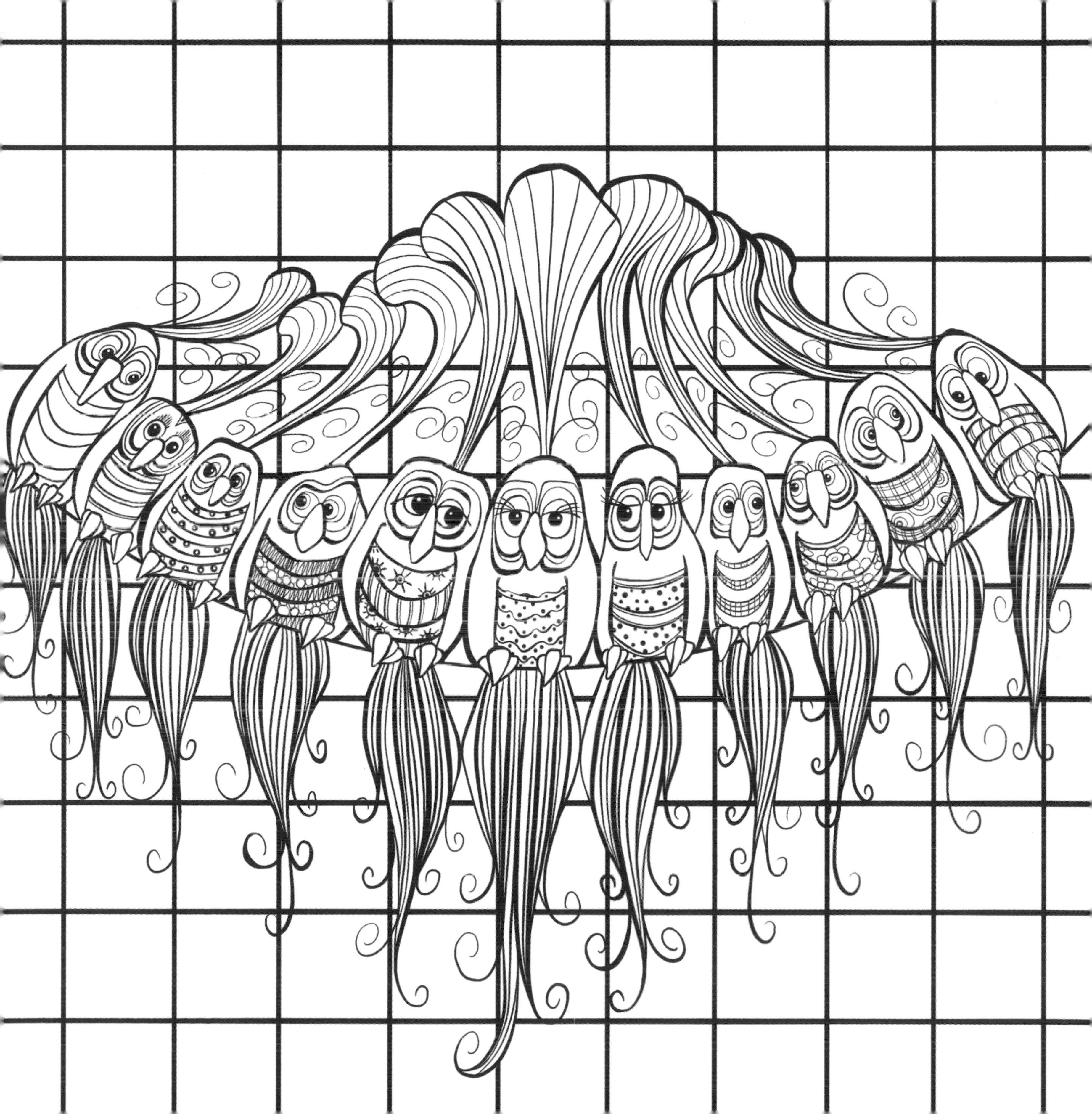

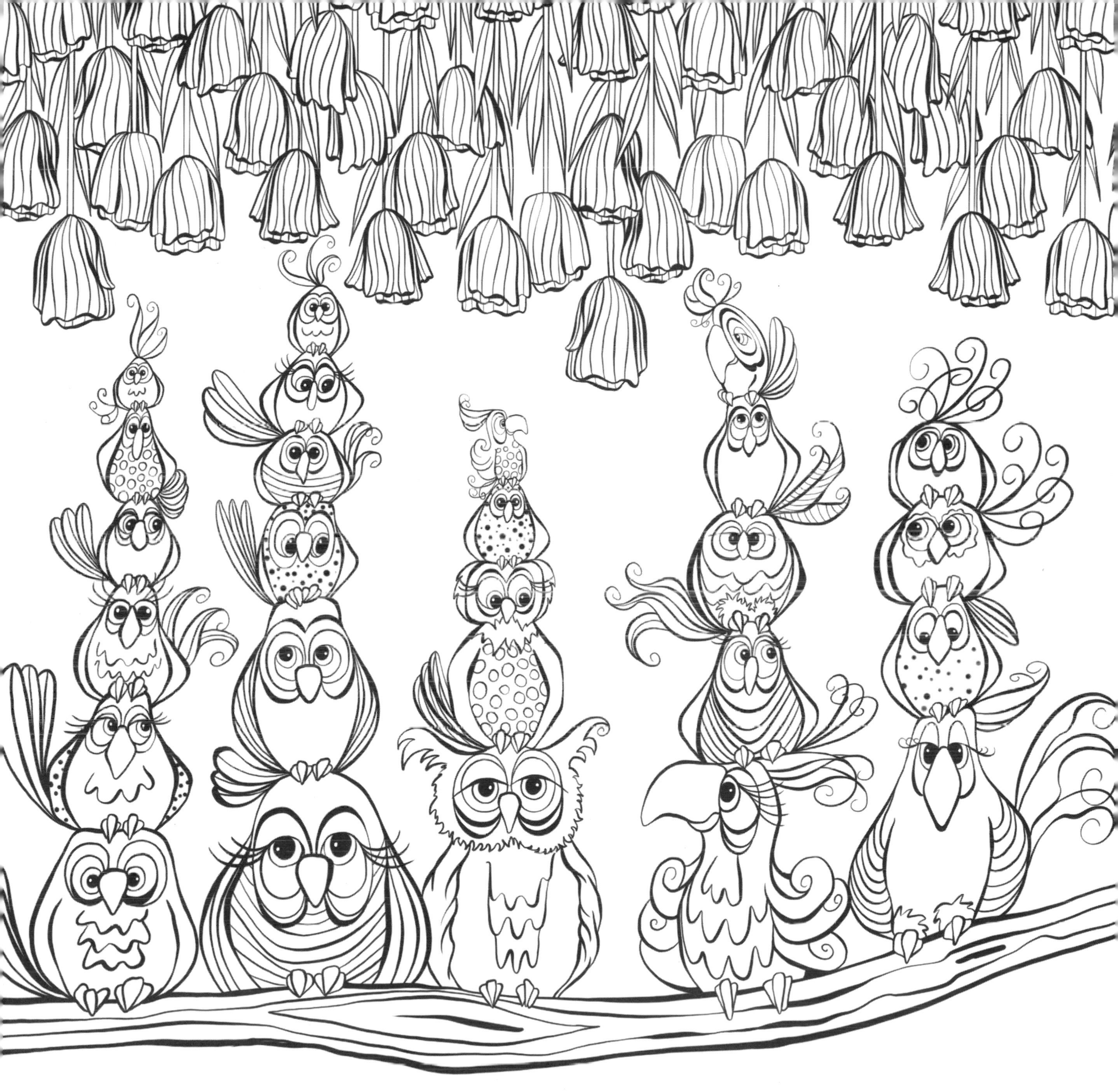

ONEY

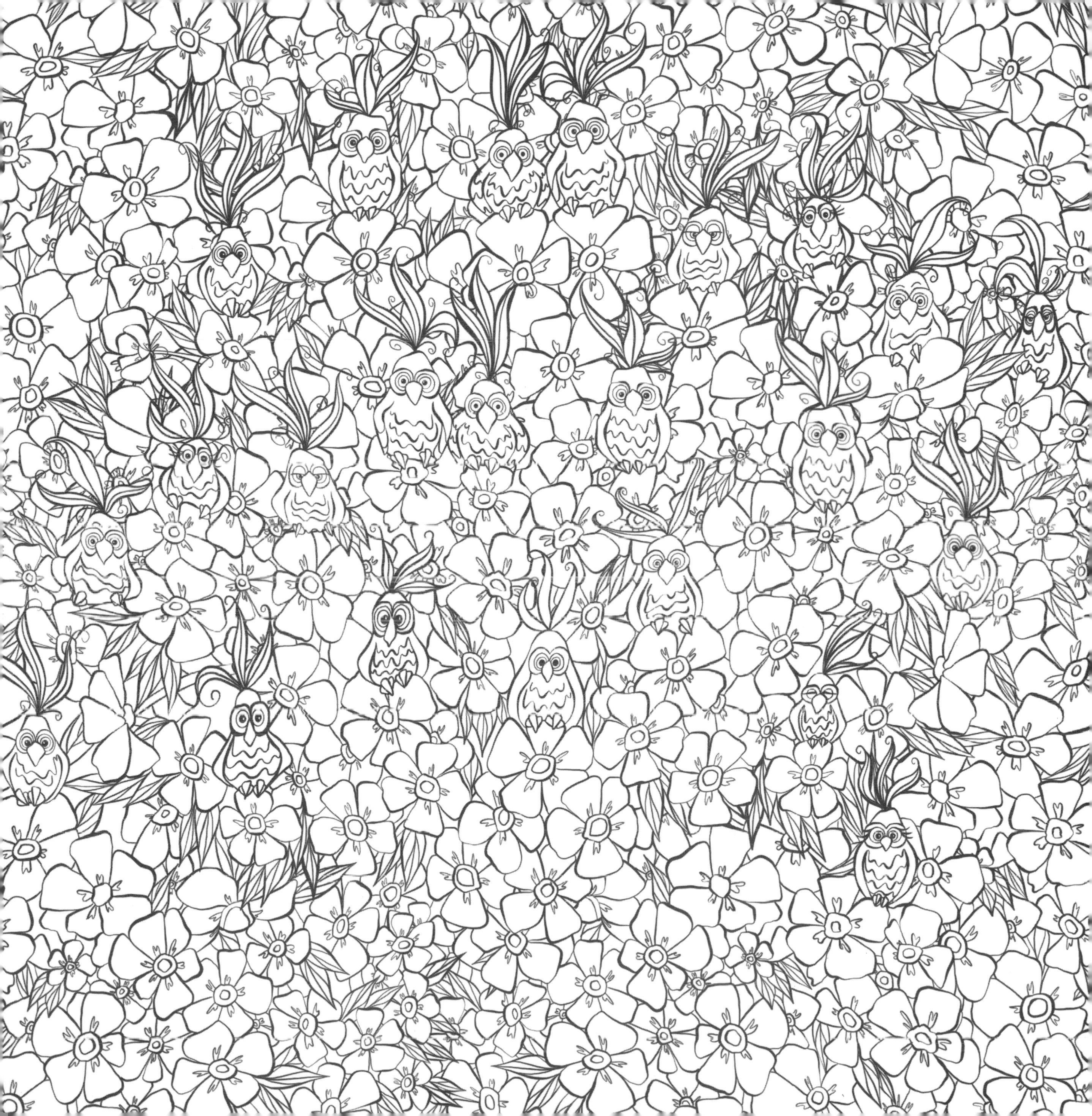

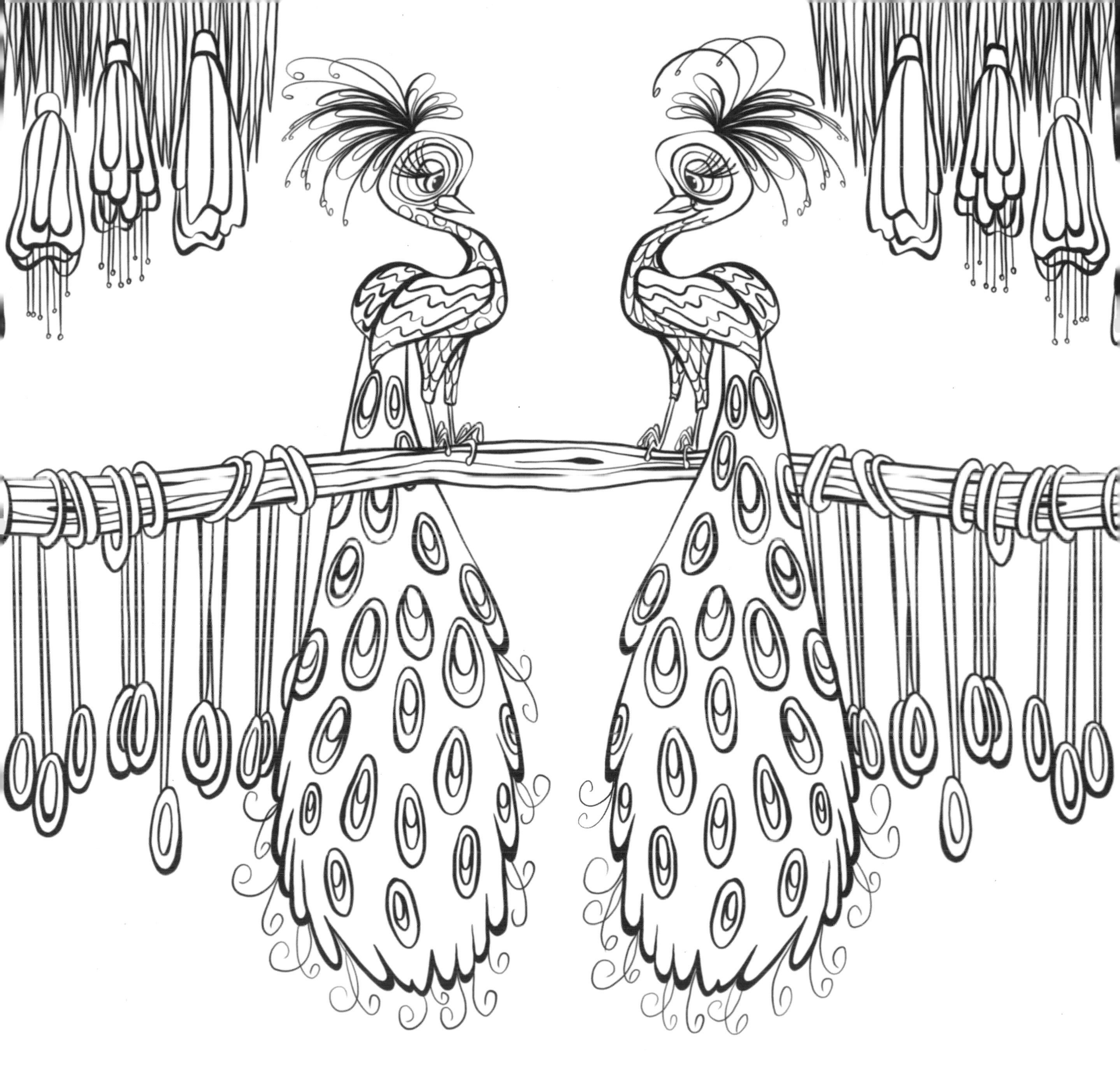